STRATEGIC STUDIES INSTITUTE

The Strategic Studies Institute (SSI) is part of the U.S. Army War College and is the strategic-level study agent for issues related to national security and military strategy with emphasis on geostrategic analysis.

The mission of SSI is to use independent analysis to conduct strategic studies that develop policy recommendations on:

- Strategy, planning, and policy for joint and combined employment of military forces;

- Regional strategic appraisals;

- The nature of land warfare;

- Matters affecting the Army's future;

- The concepts, philosophy, and theory of strategy; and,

- Other issues of importance to the leadership of the Army.

Studies produced by civilian and military analysts concern topics having strategic implications for the Army, the Department of Defense, and the larger national security community.

In addition to its studies, SSI publishes special reports on topics of special or immediate interest. These include edited proceedings of conferences and topically oriented roundtables, expanded trip reports, and quick-reaction responses to senior Army leaders.

The Institute provides a valuable analytical capability within the Army to address strategic and other issues in support of Army participation in national security policy formulation.

Strategic Studies Institute
and
U.S. Army War College Press

U.S. POLICY AND STRATEGY
TOWARD AFGHANISTAN AFTER 2014

Larry P. Goodson
Thomas H. Johnson

October 2014

*****

Comments pertaining to this report are invited and should be forwarded to: Director, Strategic Studies Institute and U.S. Army War College Press, U.S. Army War College, 47 Ashburn Drive, Carlisle, PA 17013-5010.

*****

*****

The Strategic Studies Institute and U.S. Army War College Press publishes a monthly email newsletter to update the national security community on the research of our analysts, recent and forthcoming publications, and upcoming conferences sponsored by the Institute. Each newsletter also provides a strategic commentary by one of our research analysts. If you are interested in receiving this newsletter, please subscribe on the SSI website at *www.StrategicStudiesInstitute.army.mil/newsletter*.

FOREWORD

The security relationship between the United States and Afghanistan will undergo significant change over the next year. Domestic issues in both countries will shape that new relationship, as well as regional issues within and between key neighbors of Afghanistan. During the 2014 State of the Union Address, President Barack Obama said:

> After 2014, we will support a unified Afghanistan as it takes responsibility for its own future. . . ., a small force of Americans could remain in Afghanistan with NATO allies to carry out two narrow missions: training and assisting Afghan forces, and counterterrorism operations to pursue any remnants of al Qaeda.[1]

This statement will inform U.S. policy and the new security relationship with Afghanistan from a U.S. perspective. From an Afghan perspective, the transition of the presidency from Hamid Karzai to one of the two final candidates (Ashraf Ghani Ahmadzai or Abdullah Abdullah) who competed in the June 14, 2014, second round elections will be the defining event shaping the new relationship. This monograph offers insightful analysis and practical recommendations for a strategy to shape the new U.S.–Afghanistan relationship.

As part of their research design, Dr. Larry Goodson and Dr. Thomas Johnson augmented their personal analysis with insights gathered from a wargaming workshop conducted at the U.S. Army War College's Center for Strategic Leadership and Development (CSLD) in January 2014. Subject matter experts representing military, academic, and policymaking perspectives offered thoughts on the research questions posed by the authors as they were led through the wargaming scenarios by CSLD facilitators. This broad-based exchange of ideas deepened and enriched the analysis and recommendations presented here.

The authors offer national security leaders important and timely insights, as a start-point for developing more detailed strategy and policies that will define the new U.S.–Afghanistan relationship. They ground their study in a brief analysis of the successes and failures of U.S. policy in Afghanistan since 2001. From there, they examine the changing contours of the current domestic, regional, and global security environments influencing U.S. policy and strategy choices. Relying on a "clean slate" assessment of U.S. interests and constraints emerging from this environmental scan, they identify four important U.S. national security interests that exist in and around Afghanistan. Those interests are: 1) Contain or prevent the threat of terrorist attacks on the homeland or American interests abroad; 2) Prevent the proliferation of weapons of mass destruction from the region; 3) Ensure regional stability; and, 4) Forestall rising peer competitors in the region. Finally, they conclude by offering a broad three-part strategy for post-2014 Afghanistan: 1) Finish destroying al-Qaeda; 2) Continue rebuilding Afghanistan; and, 3) Regionalize strategy.

This monograph was completed in April 2014, and therefore does not include mention of more recent developments such as the U.S.-Afghan Bilateral Security Agreement. However, the problems and themes it describes are permanent ones, and continue to present important considerations for protecting the interests of the United States and its allies in the region in the longer term.

By publishing this timely analysis in concert with the presidential leadership transition in Afghanistan, the U.S. Army War College hopes to generate an informed and reflective public debate on U.S.-Afghanistan security strategy post-2014.

Douglas C. Lovelace, Jr.

DOUGLAS C. LOVELACE, JR.
Director
Strategic Studies Institute and
U.S. Army War College Press

ENDNOTE - FOREWORD

1. President Barack Obama, State of the Union Address. Washington, DC: The White House, Office of the Press Secretary, January 28, 2014, available from *www.whitehouse.gov/the-press-office/2014/01/28/president-barack-obamas-state-union-address.*

ABOUT THE AUTHORS

LARRY P. GOODSON holds the General Dwight D. Eisenhower Chair of National Security at the U.S. Army War College, where he serves as Professor of Middle East Studies. Regularly consulted by senior government officials, in 2008-09 he served on a 4-month temporary assignment with the U.S. Central Command Assessment Team, where he focused on U.S. strategy and policy toward Afghanistan and Pakistan for General David Petraeus. As U.S. Central Command Fellow in 2004, he served as a senior adviser to General John Abizaid on Afghanistan and Pakistan. In 2002, Dr. Goodson was Technical Adviser on Elections and one of the International Election Monitors for the Emergency Loya Jirga in Afghanistan. Dr. Goodson has also held teaching appointments at Bentley College, the University of the South, the American University in Cairo, Campbell University, and the University of North Carolina-Greensboro. He has consulted with numerous U.S. Government agencies, government agencies of other countries (such as Canada), intergovernmental organizations (such as the North Atlantic Treaty Organization), and nongovernmental organizations. He has lectured on Afghanistan, Pakistan, Islam, and the Middle East at more than 100 universities, schools, and organizations, and been interviewed more than 1,000 times on those subjects by numerous media since September 11, 2001. Dr. Goodson is the author of the New York Times bestselling *Afghanistan's Endless War: State Failure, Regional Politics, and the Rise of the Taliban* (2001) and the forthcoming *Pakistan: Understanding the Dark Side of the Moon.* He contributes frequent book chapters and articles to academic journals such as the *Journal of Democracy,*

Orbis, Central Asian Survey, and *Asian Survey*, as well as opinion pieces in major news magazines and newspapers like *The New York Times, New Republic, Newsday*, and *Baltimore Sun*. He has just completed an article on the dangers of Syria's civil war sparking a region-wide upheaval in the Middle East. Dr. Goodson holds a B.A. in political science and economics, an M.A. in political science, and a Ph.D. in political science from the University of North Carolina-Chapel Hill.

THOMAS H. JOHNSON is the Research Professor and Director of the Program for Culture and Conflict Studies at the Naval Postgraduate School. He has conducted research and written about Afghanistan, South Asia, the Middle East and North Africa for over 2 decades. He has taught at the University of Southern California and the Foreign Service Institute, and frequently lectures at Service Academies. Before joining the faculty of the Naval Postgraduate School, he served on the research faculty of George Mason University. He regularly conducts field research in Afghanistan and South Asia. He served as the Counter-insurgency Advisor to the Commander of Task Force Kandahar (Gen. Jon Vance). Dr. Johnson has written publications appearing in the *American Political Science Review, International Security, Journal of Politics, Orbis: A Journal of World Affairs, Central Asian Survey, Military Review, China and Eurasian Forum Quarterly, Middle East Journal, Small Wars and Insurgencies, Strategic Insights, Public Opinion, The Brown Journal of World Affairs, Strategic Review, Politikon: South African Journal of Political Science, The Historian, Journal of Modern African Studies*, as well as numerous scholarly edited volumes and texts. His commentaries have appeared in numerous media outlets to include *The Washington Post, Atlantic*

Monthly, Wall Street Journal, Chicago Tribune, Baltimore Sun, Globe and Mail, Toronto Star, Correio Braziliense (Brazil), Newsday, Newsweek and on *PBS NewsHour, CNN's Christianne Amanpour Show, CBS, BBC, CNBC, KCBS, KQED, National Public Radio's All Things Considered* and the *Morning Edition* and *Voice of America.*

SUMMARY

As the United States continues to withdraw troops from and prepares to leave Afghanistan, Afghanistan faces multifaceted and significant challenges of governance, economy, security, and regional dynamics. These are all occurring within the context of the potential for an expanded civil war when international forces leave the country. It is time to refocus from the conflict itself and ask hard, but realistic, strategic and policy questions as to the future of Afghanistan, and what role, if any, the United States should play in shaping that future.

After nearly 13 years, over 2,200 lives lost, and over U.S.$650 billion spent since the United States began its air campaign against Afghanistan's Taliban in October 2001, the end of the long American military campaign in Afghanistan appears to be in sight. Despite the cost and challenges, the reality that Afghanistan still ranks consistently in the bottom 10 countries for human development and corruption, and the uneven but clear progress that the country has made in many areas, the United States will soon scale down its involvement in Afghanistan, and quite possibly pull all uniformed military forces out of Afghanistan quite rapidly. Additionally, the widely reported corruption that exists throughout the Afghan government, the resilient Taliban-led insurgency, and a litany of Western blunders, mishaps, and tragedies have all helped to undermine Western interest in the Afghan War. Recent surveys suggest that public support for the war is dwindling in Western and North Atlantic Treaty Organization (NATO) member countries, with 75 percent of European respondents and 68 percent of U.S. respondents supporting either withdrawal or immediate troop reductions according to the German Marshall Fund Annual Transatlantic Trends Survey. Alternatively, perhaps the declining interest in Afghanistan is connected to a widespread popular and policymaker belief, especially since the 2011 Abbottabad raid (Operation NEPTUNE SPEAR) that killed Osama bin Laden, that U.S. and NATO war aims in Afghanistan have been achieved, or at least achieved to a sufficient degree given the current fiscal and political climate.

This monograph answers six key questions about U.S. policy and strategy for Afghanistan:

1. Did the United States have or develop critical national interests in Afghanistan and its immediate neighborhood on or because of the events of September 11, 2001?

2. Was overall U.S. strategy to pursue those interests successful and appropriate?

3. What outside conditions shaping U.S. involvement in Afghanistan exist now?

4. Do new vital and/or important national interests not met by our earlier strategies exist in this region?

5. What strategy(s) should the United States adopt or emphasize to achieve any vital and/or important national interests in/around Afghanistan?

6. What risks and challenges are associated with new policies and/or strategies?

The authors' answers to these questions provide the foundation for recommendations to U.S. policy and strategy in order to achieve current and future national security interests in the regions that Afghanistan straddles.

U.S. POLICY AND STRATEGY TOWARD AFGHANISTAN AFTER 2014

Introduction.

The United States will soon reach a major inflection point in its long and trying post-September 11, 2001 (9/11) engagement with Afghanistan. In order to make certain that our policy and strategy going forward allows us to achieve key national interests in the most effective way, we must carefully consider the past policies and strategies with regard to Afghanistan and the surrounding region, the current conditions that constrain and influence our capabilities, as well as overall U.S. global interests.

Afghanistan has not been a success story for the United States to date; nor has it been an unmitigated disaster. Some national interests have been achieved, but the cost in so doing has been high, and it has taken a long time. As with any military action, covert operation, diplomatic initiative, or development project; accidents, cost overruns, excesses, inefficiencies, and just plain mistakes have undermined public confidence and called into question our overall Afghanistan policy. The deep-seated and chronic corruption and graft of the Afghan government and its rampant inefficiency has also proven problematic. Future policy and strategy toward Afghanistan must take into account not only the successes already achieved, but also the costs and shortcomings incurred in achieving those successes.

National Interests after 9/11.[1]

Prior to 9/11, American policy toward Afghanistan had been largely to ignore what was a Central Asian backwater, outside of American alliance structures and essentially a remote and deeply underdeveloped extension of the Soviet Central Asian republics. Indeed, for virtually all of Afghan history with the exception of the Soviet occupation period (1979-89), U.S. policy toward the country and its surrounding region was to treat it as a minor and peripheral interest.[2] Little could occur there of consequence to the United States. After the attacks on the United States on 9/11, immediate policy changes toward Afghanistan and the terrorists harboring there were enacted, especially with regard to the Afghan Taliban.

The year 1979 proved to be a watershed in U.S. relations with Afghanistan and the South Asian region. The Soviet invasion of Afghanistan on Christmas Day 1979 presented the United States with an opportunity to "bleed" the Soviet Union, which had become a persistent and unremitting rival during the Cold War. Also, the Islamic Revolution in Iran and dissolution of the Central Treaty Organization in 1979 combined with the Soviet invasion of Afghanistan to prompt the 1980 Carter Doctrine and limited covert proxy war fought by the United States in Afghanistan in the 1980s. Despite that, the United States had no truly vital national interests in Afghanistan. The covert war was pursued as a strategy in support of what became known in 1985 as the Reagan Doctrine, which committed the United States to aid anti-communist fighters in the developing world against Soviet-supported dictatorial regimes. This, of course, was in direct contradiction to the Brezhnev Doctrine which called on the Soviet Union to directly support any fledgling Socialist regime on its borders.

Evidence for our limited policy interests in Afghanistan was abundant at the end of the 1980s. After a decade of successful covert and other operations contributed to driving the Soviet Union out of Afghanistan in 1989, we reverted to our traditional posture toward the country and treated it as a minor backwater as we turned our foreign policy focus elsewhere. Afghanistan staggered on throughout the 1990s, bedeviled by persistent civil war between rapacious warlords and Islamist Taliban, with some involvement of outside actors. Although the United States was aware of the increasingly dangerous al-Qaeda terrorists operating in and from Afghanistan during the latter half of the 1990s, we were unsuccessful at eliminating or containing that threat, until 9/11 forced a change to U.S. policy virtually overnight. Two vital national interests immediately came into being:

1. Destroy al-Qaeda and degrade its network of support, both to exact retribution and to prevent its ability to do further harm to the United States; and,

2. Make it impossible for anti-American terrorists to operate again from Afghanistan or its immediate neighborhood.

Operation ENDURING FREEDOM (OEF) beginning in 2001 as part of the broader Global War on Terror (GWOT) was the most obvious manifestation of a U.S. policy change toward Afghanistan that now elevated the country and its problems to the very forefront of U.S. foreign policy concerns and national interests. The foremost objective of U.S. policy in this era was to destroy anti-American terrorist organizations, especially those that might pursue weapons of mass destruction (WMD), and to degrade their sources of support in countries that were perceived to be aligned against U.S. interests. That policy interest led the United States to invade Iraq in 2003 and topple the Saddam Hussein regime there, as well as to attack primarily Islamist terrorists in various locations around the world, especially Pakistan, Yemen, the Horn of Africa, North Africa, and Southeast Asia. These approaches appeared to follow the 2002 *National Security Strategy* that emphasized we would "strengthen alliances to defeat global terrorism and work to prevent attacks against us and our friends."[3]

Strategy after 9/11.

Strategy is the calculated relationship between ends, ways, and means, with the risk of the variable being affected when that relationship is unbalanced. Strategy can be measured by its feasibility, acceptability, and suitability, as follows:

- Suitability — will its attainment accomplish the effect desired (relates to objective)?
- Feasibility — can the action be accomplished by the means available (relates to concept)?
- Acceptability — are the consequences of cost justified by the importance of the effect desired (relates to resources/concept)?[4]

The challenge posed by the 9/11 attack on the United States was in rapidly developing an effective strategy(s) to achieve the radically changed policy objectives outlined earlier.

Realistically, however, the U.S. national security architecture was not constructed to respond to the threat posed by Islamist terrorists or the nation-building activities that our military interventions in Afghanistan and Iraq necessitated. Almost from the very beginning of our increased involvement in Afghanistan, strategic incoherence dominated our approach. Ultimately, nation-building[5] in Afghanistan (and Iraq) seemed to involve three primary lines of effort: security, governance, and economic development.[6] Each of those lines of effort came to be led by a particular part and sometimes more than one part of the U.S. Government.

Over time, four major strategic approaches would be adopted for Afghanistan. From the beginning, we focused on counterterrorism (CT) against the al-Qaeda and Taliban who attacked us and/or the Kabul government that we put in place of the Taliban early in OEF. The intelligence community, especially the Central Intelligence Agency (CIA), and the military special operations community, primarily led this strategy, which focused on "High-Value Targets" (HVTs). As the country of Afghanistan was essentially underdeveloped and without a functioning government when we intervened, we also devised a strategic approach that emphasized nation-building activities, despite the fact that President George W. Bush had campaigned for the presidency in 2000 against nation-building. No part of the U.S. Government mastered state-building (or governmental and institutional development) and economic development, so the State Department had the lead in engaging with the rest of the international community in these areas. Not surprisingly, given the widespread needs and institutional inadequacies inside Afghanistan, plus the multitude of outside actors that accepted responsibility for different components of the nation-building process, progress was uneven and slow. Security sector reform was also a component of Afghan institution building on which the U.S. military eventually had most of the lead, while it was also engaged in combat operations in Afghanistan.[7] Later, after the apparent success of counterinsurgency (COIN) operations in Iraq, the United States surged forces into Afghanistan and attempted a similar approach there, meaning that elements of the Department of Defense (DoD) had a hand in four strategic approaches.[8]

The cost of this complex, overlapping, and oftentimes divergent infrastructure for success in Afghanistan paradoxically made that success harder to achieve. The heavy emphasis on CT efforts, replicated in Iraq, meant we abandoned the moral high ground almost from the outset in order to pursue frequently classified "capture-kill" operations and then to imprison individuals captured thereby in "black" detention/rendition facilities in Afghanistan, third countries, or Guantanamo Bay.

We also supported numerous warlords and delayed the Disarmament, Demobilization, and Reintegration (DDR) of their militias in order to utilize their forces against the Taliban, who had fled across the Durand Line into Pakistan, putting them initially outside the reach of American CT efforts. Our nation-building efforts were hamstrung by a lack of commitment, inadequate institutional capacity, and the huge challenges posed by Afghanistan's virtually complete absence of a functional infrastructure due to its long years of destructive war. Moreover, in the first half of the 2000s, we allowed a division of labor of the nation-building mission to a United Nations that we clearly held in disdain, as well as organizations like the World Bank and Asian Development Bank, plus bilateral partners. Clumsy but well-intended initial efforts to repair, rebuild, or even reinvent Afghanistan after a generation's worth of war were soon overtaken by the relentless pace of the U.S. intervention in Iraq, which relegated Afghanistan to a back burner. Centrifugal forces associated more with localism than nationalism had become resurgent during the many years of war, and in the absence of functioning institutions provided the foundation for Afghanistan's next chapter. Thus, even as a government was established, constitution written, ministries reinvigorated, and trust funds created, the Afghan government became an out-of-control hodgepodge of kleptocratic, incestuous, and corrupt thugs who plundered the treasury of its foreign largesse for their own, oftentimes dubious, ends. Inevitably, and over time, the Afghan government proved its ineptitude. The insurgencies and violent opposition it engendered grew more intense. Therefore, military operations to defeat the opposition grew more complex and required more troops, and cross-border efforts to strike the Taliban in their sanctuaries began in 2004 and leaped in intensity in 2008.

Notwithstanding all the difficulties, most Americans have come to believe that our Afghanistan strategies have achieved our post-9/11 national interests, or at least as much as they are likely to. Al-Qaeda has been the object of an unremitting capture/kill campaign for over 12 years, with virtually all of the top leadership of what was always a very small group taken off the battlefield prior to the 2011 Abbottabad Raid that caused the death of Osama bin Laden. Although Ayman Al-Zawahiri assumed the leadership of al-Qaeda after Bin Laden's death, most Americans felt that the Abbottabad Raid meant that the core al-Qaeda organization was no longer a serious threat to the United States and that retribution for 9/11 had finally been exacted. As for making Afghanistan no longer hospitable to anti-American terrorists, that was supposed to be accomplished by the institutional and economic development of the country that was to occur by virtue of the Bonn Process and the repeated international conferences aimed at raising funding for Afghanistan development. Unfortunately, the Bonn Process provided for a model of graduated transition to constitutional government that would take time and was not well understood by many Afghans. This essentially meant that while Security Sector Reform and other institutional developments were being pursued as long-term projects, human capital development would need at least a generation to begin to offset the lost generation of the 1980s and 1990s. As the nation-building process dragged on and grew more expensive, however, it also became increasingly obvious that most Afghans who engaged in anti-American violence saw themselves as resistance fighters or were pursuing violence for economic gain or, if they were inspired by religious ideology, perceived themselves as engaged in a defensive jihad.[9] Thus, there seems to be little likelihood that significant attacks on the American homeland will originate from Afghanistan again.

Despite the success (or exhaustion) achieved by U.S. strategies in securing American interests in Afghanistan—albeit at great expense and to some extent imperfectly—the Afghan War has been our nation's longest war and it has inevitably led to changed conditions in the region, which arguably have created new national interests there. This mission creep is a by-product of a changing regional environment that has seen the emergence of a multipolar scramble for Central Asia in which all the regional powers are taking part,[10] usually pursuing divergent interests.

Meanwhile, a global economic downturn has spurred on not only the regional competition for Afghan and Central Asian resources but exacerbated Western publics' war-weariness with the Afghan imbroglio (indeed, all military interventions, if the recent disquiet over Syria, Ukraine, and Iraq are anything to go by!). Moreover, the apparently successful use of drones, Special Forces, and other light footprint technologies and approaches in Afghanistan and elsewhere suggest to many that such national interests, as do exist in Afghanistan's neighborhood, might be managed by those means.

Outside Conditions.

Before turning our attention to post-2014 U.S. interest, policies, and strategies, we should consider how the past 13 years have changed conditions shaping U.S. involvement in Afghanistan. At least four major factors deserve attention: the modern-day multipolarity of the region (the "new Great Game"); the war-weariness among Western publics; the technological and military advances that have made counterterrorism less labor-intensive, reducing the required footprint; and the fragile economic conditions across the globe. Some of these conditions may serve as constraints on U.S. or other outside action, although presumably they do not affect fundamental U.S. interests. As constraints, however, they deserve attention.

Today, the United States plays the dominant role in the region, but a rising China, emerging India, active Pakistan, reemerging Russia, troubled Iran, and other regional players all are actively engaged in Afghanistan, as well as multilateral and non-governmental organizations. While not all of these countries and outside actors have divergent interests, enough do such that Afghanistan has become a playing field in a multipolar struggle between regional and great powers.[11]

China and India are increasingly competing in a rivalry for Asian dominance. The more obvious manifestation of that competition has been the naval and maritime race for supremacy in the Indian Ocean and littoral areas of Southeast and East Asia, but desire for natural resources and geographic position have brought China and India into Central Asia as well. China has invested more than $5 billion in Afghanistan to date, primarily in the Aynak copper mine and in winning bids to develop oil tracts in Faryab and Sar-i-Pul. India has a broader and deeper relationship with Afghanistan, having signed a strategic partnership in 2011. India has also built roads and other infrastructure in Afghanistan, refurbished and upgraded the Chabahar port in Iran in 2009 and the road from there to the Afghan border town of Zaranj in order to weaken Afghan dependence on Pakistani access to the outside world, and sponsored Afghanistan's membership in the South Asian Association for Regional Cooperation (SAARC) since 2006. Indian companies have made more than $2 billion in investments in Afghanistan, especially the successful bid for the bulk of the Hajigak iron ore in Bamiyan. The Hajigak bid is the centerpiece of an expected $10.7 billion in investment over the next 30 years, as well as more than one billion dollars in aid since 2002.

Pakistan has neither the resources as India or China nor the same strategic approach toward Afghanistan. Nonetheless, Pakistan considers itself to be the immediate neighbor that has suffered the most due to Afghanistan's turbulent history and is thus most entitled to a stable Afghanistan that is favorably disposed to it. That is, Pakistan wants a Pashtun government in Kabul that will not pursue policies that it considers inimical to its interests. Therefore, it intends to use the Taliban as its cat's paw in Afghanistan, either as a militia in a future civil war, or as a partner in a future Afghan government. Similarly, Iran wants to preserve its influence in western Afghanistan, where there is not a strong enough agent to contend for power or power-sharing in Kabul. Iran has helped to develop its own route into Afghanistan in concert with India, as mentioned already, in order to offset Pakistan's influence through Afghanistan's southern and eastern Pashtun belt.

Russia has less direct influence in Afghanistan, but it fears another resurgence of militant Islamism there and it has extensive investment in the oil and gas infrastructure in the other Central Asian states north of Afghanistan. Russia also fears the expansion of Chinese influence in Central Asia. Russia, Iran, and Pakistan have all become important transit routes for Afghanistan's heroin, and not surprisingly, have developed large populations of drug addicts. Thus, all three countries want Afghanistan's drug economy brought under control. Russia's former satellites, Afghanistan's northern neighbors Tajikistan, Uzbekistan, and Turkmenistan (as well as Kyrgyzstan and Kazakhstan), also suffer from the drug trafficking and the possibility of rising Islamist militancy, plus they are caught geographically in the scramble for Central Asian gas and oil resources, with the prospect of pipelines and transit corridors coming from all points of the compass and all major regional players.

The Gulf Arab states have little direct influence inside Afghanistan but subscribe to the proverbial wisdom that "the enemy of my enemy is my friend," meaning the Gulf Arab states generally oppose advances to Iran's interests in Afghanistan. Finally, the United States and its NATO partners have invested far more money in Afghanistan than anyone else, but now face a heightened war-weariness that has caused a loss of political will to remain there.

This war-weariness means that the Afghan imbroglio appears to be reaching its end in terms of significant involvement of major Western powers. Public opinion data from across NATO countries—and the United States is especially relevant—show unequivocally that Western publics consider the Afghan War to be complete. Western support for the Afghan War had declined steadily from 2003 onward, but almost from the beginning of the Obama administration in early 2009 popular opinion passed the threshold of more people being opposed than favored the deployment of troops there.[12] Since then, popular opinion has continued on its downward trend, accelerating somewhat after the May 2011 Abbottabad Raid that killed Osama Bin Laden. As the poll results reveal, 66% of Americans believe the Afghan War is not worth fighting now, although public opinion remains divided about whether to remove all troops there.[13]

The 2012 Transatlantic Trends Survey of the German Marshall Fund showed that 68% of Americans and 75% of survey respondents from European Union countries believed then "that troop levels should be reduced or troops should be withdrawn altogether from Afghanistan."[14] However, the 2013 Survey showed that 53% of Europeans and 54% of Americans favored keeping some troops in Afghanistan to train the Afghan army and police.[15] The timetable already in place for a gradual drawdown of Western troops means that

Western unease about the continuing involvement in Afghanistan may be somewhat mollified by the expectation that the war is gradually coming to a close. Some support remains for limited troop deployments into the future, as already indicated; that support seems to be motivated by a continuing concern over the threat of Islamist terrorism against Americans and not due to geopolitics or other possible national interests. The mixed feelings concerning Afghanistan by the American public were on wide display during the raging debate over the release from Taliban captivity of SGT Bowe Bergdahl. Bergdahl, of the U.S. Army, was held captive by the Taliban-aligned Haqqani network in Afghanistan from June 2009 until his release in May 2014. The release was part of a controversial five-for-one prisoner trade with the Taliban that the Obama administration secretly orchestrated with the Taliban through Qatar.

In 2012, Washington announced a highly publicized "pivot to the Pacific," or strategic rebalancing of American diplomatic and defense focus onto the Western Pacific Rim, signaling that America's post-2001 fixation on the Islamic World and its threatening radicals was over.[16] Yet, those radicals remain dangerous and they still appear intent on striking the United States and U.S. interests. Moreover, the worsening Syrian and Iraqi civil wars and the apparent continuing march of the Iranian regime toward a viable nuclear weapons program present the United States with national security challenges in the Islamic World that cannot be ignored. "Light footprint" military and intelligence approaches straight from the ancient wisdom of Kautilya[17] provide ways and means for dealing with those challenges, but at significant philosophical and moral cost for the United States.[18]

At least some national security threats may be different in nature than traditional threats, perhaps because they emanate from non-state actors with at least aspirations of utilizing weapons of mass destruction. Or, perhaps U.S. capabilities and/or doctrine are such that the best response to these threats is non-traditional, leaning less on conventional armies and navies (or even strategic nuclear forces) and more on armed unmanned aerial vehicles (UAVs), cyber attacks, direct action (i.e., targeted killings), clandestine operations, information operations, and leveraging of unique capabilities possessed by allied and/or friendly countries.

A significant challenge, though, is that nontraditional ways of war may still constitute acts of war. What does that mean for the widely reported cross-border drone operations from Afghanistan into Pakistan? Pakistan is a Major Non-NATO Ally (MNNA) that also provides the cheapest and most effective supply lines by which the United States continues to supply its forces in landlocked Afghanistan. Given these circumstances, no formal mechanism by the U.S. government to provide a legal basis for military or paramilitary action inside Pakistan has been announced, although many Americans might view such acts and approaches to be appropriate. The strategic divide in the American approach to Afghanistan between CT and state building combined with the ability of most of the Taliban and al-Qaeda fighters to escape to Pakistan in the early stages of the Afghan War led inevitably to U.S. cross-border operations in Pakistan, an MNNA country, sometimes in conjunction with the Pakistani government (although not acknowledged to the Pakistani public) and sometimes without Pakistani approval or foreknowledge.

This seeming conundrum, which some would call duplicity, occurred because Pakistan viewed the asymmetric actors operating from its territory as its only effective offensive tools in its long-standing struggle with India. Thus, Pakistan wanted to maintain them and even use them against rising Indian influence within Afghanistan, but maintaining those actors caused problems with the Americans inside Afghanistan to whom Pakistan was ostensibly allied. Moreover, the grudging decision by Pakistani President Pervez Musharraf in 2001 to be "with" rather than "against" the United States in Afghanistan caused many of the Islamist terrorist groups within Pakistan to turn against the Pakistani government.[19] Consequently, at least some of the Pakistani national security leadership wanted the United States to attack certain targets within Pakistan, most notably those anti-Pakistani government Islamist militants operating out of the quasi-autonomous Federally Administered Tribal Areas (FATA) that abut Afghanistan, even as those same leaders kept certain other asymmetric actors from being captured or killed, primarily by keeping them in secure locations outside of the FATA. Thus, since 2004 the United States has conducted more than 370 drone strikes causing at least 2,000 deaths inside Pakistan,[20] even as the Afghan insurgency against the Karzai government intensified, bolstered by its cross-border sanctuary and support. The United States has also conducted cross-border raids, most notably Operation NEPTUNE SPEAR that killed Osama bin Laden in May 2011.

This method of counterterrorism, which relies primarily on unconventional forces, clandestine intelligence gathering, and new technology, has proven to be effective in this unique situation.[21] President Barack Obama embraced this approach to warfare early in his first term in office, accelerating a program of striking Pakistani-based militants with missiles fired from drones that had begun under President Bush in June 2004 and continued very selectively until the latter half of 2008, when the Bush administration ramped up the pace of these strikes, more than doubling the number of attacks in the last 6 months of 2008 than had occurred in the previous 4 years. The Obama administration introduced a surge of U.S. troops into Afghanistan starting in 2009, but its tactic of choice was the cross-border drone strike into Pakistani territory, with President Obama himself reportedly personally approving the targets of the strikes.[22]

"Light footprint" CT of this sort that has been used in Pakistan (and elsewhere) is seductive to policymakers, especially in an austere fiscal climate when the largest segment of the U.S. Government's discretionary spending has been its defense budget. Cheaper tools and capabilities of war may move America farther and farther away from the traditional "American way of war" into an era of near-permanent, silent war, tucked away from public scrutiny in the shadows.[23] If so, Afghanistan and its neighborhood has already become the arena for America's new "light footprint" approach to addressing national security threats, which presumably may be sufficient for dealing with those now-reduced threats and allowing American military forces to be deployed elsewhere.

Moreover, eroding economic conditions now exist that constrain U.S. policy and strategy choices and tip American leaders toward more limited approaches to war. The global economic downturn that began in late-2007 both spread and persisted, creating an austere economic climate in the United States that combined with expensive wars paid for by supplemental appropriations and growing entitlement burdens on the shrinking fiscal side of the budget. By 2014, the economic realities were such that military spending — the largest discretionary item in the budget — was set for a substantial cut. In particular, the ground forces (especially the Army) face significant cuts in overall strength, as the rebalancing to the Asia-Pacific combines with the Air-Sea Battle concept to motivate most military spending on the expensive aircraft and ships of the Air Force and Navy.[24]

Thus, if new wars must be fought in the near term, they cannot be fought in the same way as the wars of the first decade of the 21st century, as the military structure will not exist with which to do so. Moreover, the expensive and seemingly interminable nation-building operations conducted in Afghanistan and Iraq no longer appear to be sustainable by U.S. military and other government assets. Indeed, the overall weakening of many national economies, especially those of practically every NATO country involved in Afghanistan, has further reduced public willingness to fund an ongoing war or nation-building effort there. To the extent that certain national security interests remain in Afghanistan, less costly ways will have to be found to achieve those interests.

As has already been detailed, initial U.S. interests were largely achieved by expensive, poorly synchronized, often redundant strategic approaches in Afghanistan. Future strategic approaches, in a time of greater economic austerity and after the longest war in American history, are no longer deemed to be necessary by the American public. Simply put, most Americans no longer believe having troops or extensive investments in Afghanistan are worth it.

Current National Interests.

Four important national security interests now exist in and around Afghanistan:

1. Contain or prevent the threat of terrorist attacks on the homeland or American interests abroad;

2. Prevent the proliferation of WMD from the region;

3. Ensure regional stability; and,

4. Forestall rising peer competitors in the region.

The primary national interest that American involvement in Afghanistan has pursued since 9/11 has been national security, as both the CT approaches toward individual terrorists and insurgents and the organizations to which they belong, and the state-building approaches toward Afghan institutions, were all meant to advance U.S. national security. Now, al-Qaeda in the Afghanistan region is a hollow shell of its former self, requiring little in the way of continued military attention. Afghan nation-building has proven to be both exceedingly unpopular with the public and unlikely to ripen quickly enough to be a successful strategy. Both tasks are unfinished, but neither of them is important enough to warrant continued deep involvement by the United States, and both of them really represent ways to achieve U.S. national security interests in Afghanistan.

On the other hand, the rising regional competition between Asian powers (China, Russia, and India) and regional powers (Pakistan, Iran, and Saudi Arabia) has important ramifications for the United States. Thus, four national security interests now exist in and around Afghanistan. First, protecting U.S. national security by containing or preventing the threat of terrorist attacks on the homeland or American interests abroad remains important, even if the likelihood of that threat emanating from Afghanistan or its neighborhood has declined. In particular, destroying al-Qaeda and other violent Islamist organizations operating near Afghanistan remains an important priority, but al-Qaeda in this region is so degraded today that this task only requires a limited CT capability. Likewise, Afghanistan still must be rebuilt, but only insofar as it helps insulate Afghanistan from further threatening behavior toward U.S. interests, and/or as an enabler to the CT strategy. Neither destroying al-Qaeda nor rebuilding Afghanistan should be considered distinct interests of the United States, but at best are possible ways to achieve those interests.

Second, although Afghanistan has long been a remote backwater on the international stage, it is now surrounded by nuclear powers. Four of the powers (Russia, China, India, and Pakistan) already possess nuclear weapons, while Iran is inching closer to nuclear weapons status, raising the risk level if regional instability leads to open conflict. Pakistan, through its early efforts to develop nuclear weapons and then the revelations in 2004 surrounding the activities of A. Q. Khan; Iran, more recently as it has upped the level of its nuclear program; Russia, as a supplier of fissile material and nuclear engineering knowledge to Iran; and China, as a supplier of fissile material and nuclear engineering knowledge to Pakistan—all have been involved in nuclear proliferation. It cannot be ruled out that any or all of these states might engage in future nuclear proliferation.[25] This threat cannot be ignored by the United States, especially given the prospect of nuclear proliferation in a region swarming with Islamist radicals, some of whom have a long-standing desire to attack the West.

The multipolar regional environment in and around Afghanistan today makes regional stability there more important than ever. The primary national interest motivating our continued direct involvement in Afghanistan is the possibility of spillover violence from the modern multipolar struggle for influence among the major powers involved there. Two of the powers (India and Pakistan) have a long history of violent conflict, increasing the likelihood of regional instability. India had a long relationship with Russia's predecessor, the Soviet Union, while Pakistan has had a similarly long relationship with China, both major actors in the region. Given the rivalries and divergent interests that exist between these and other countries, potential alliance structures may develop that would make conflict between these powers more likely.

Given the historical rivalry between India and Pakistan, and the competition for Asian supremacy between China, Russia, and India, the prospects for regional instability are significant. As noted earlier, all of those countries also possess nuclear arsenals, and Iran has been busily pursuing a nuclear capability of its own, meaning that all the large countries in Afghanistan's neighborhood are or soon will be nuclear weapons states, raising the stakes of regional instability to a dangerously high level. While stability might be ensured if one or a combination of the regional powers rose to dominate the region, such almost certainly could not be achieved without destabilizing the region. U.S. interests are not advanced by having stability ensured by the rise of a successful peer competitor in the area (especially Russia or China, either of whom are pursuing interests at variance with important U.S. interests elsewhere). Achieving the final two interests will be challenging, as they require maintaining enough presence far from home to ensure enough stability in a region where several powerful competitors are competing with each other in pursuit of divergent interests, while not settling for allowing one of the regional competitors to emerge triumphant through a misplaced desire to avoid the cost of presence by way of a proxy. Afghanistan becoming the arena for a "proxy war" between Pakistan/China and India/Russia is probably the worst case scenario for the region.

At most, the first interest is important, but the direct threat to U.S. national security is low. The second interest is more important, even vital, if nuclear weapons are used or become insecure. Finally, the last two interests are important but connected to a larger geo-political puzzle for the United States. Given that no critical, vital national security interests now exist in Afghanistan (as the nuclear threat seems distant and not directed at the United States), it will be difficult to motivate the American public to remain engaged in Afghanistan in an extensive way, especially since the last 12 years have seen significant changes in Afghanistan and its region, among the broader Islamic World, and globally.

War-weariness and the rise of other threats to national security interests have gradually merged to move Afghanistan back to its traditional spot on the back burner of U.S. foreign policy concerns. As such, unless the strategic and economic environments shift again, there is little to no chance that the U.S. Government can continue to spend large sums of money or deploy more than a tiny fraction of the forces that have been used in Afghanistan over the past 12 years in the post-2014 time period. Moreover, the United States encouraged NATO to commit to the Afghanistan mission through the International Security Assistance Force (ISAF), which eventually expanded to become a 49-country coalition.[26] Most of these countries have now extended their involvement in Afghanistan far beyond the time that public opinion will support. All of this means that as the national security interest of combating terrorism in Afghanistan fades away, probably only two important national interests remain, which are to ensure regional stability and forestall rising peer competitors in the region. While both interests are important, neither can be considered vital after a long and grinding war that has lost its popularity with the American people.

New Strategies.

The United States now must adjust its strategies given changed domestic, regional, and global conditions; flaws in our earlier strategies; and current U.S. policy goals for Afghanistan and its immediate region. Our existing strategies do not address our present interests and are not sustainable. While they have contributed to the achievement, at least in part, of post-9/11 U.S. interests in Afghanistan, they have been expensive and they do not address the new interests. To pursue the current interests at a reasonable cost, given Afghanistan's relative distance from the United States but closeness to the Asian powers, we recommend a three-part strategy for post-2014 Afghanistan, as follows: 1) Finish destroying al-Qaeda; 2) Continue rebuilding Afghanistan; and 3) Regionalize strategy.

The first two pillars of a post-2014 strategy basically require reducing the current U.S. involvement and approach to Afghanistan. Many operational details will need to be managed with a high degree of sensitivity to reduce the U.S. presence in a way that advances rather than retards U.S. interests. Such details exceed the scope of this analysis, but it would be preferable for reductions in U.S. presence to be well planned rather than precipitate — certainly it would be best to avoid any "helicopters on the Embassy roof" moments.[27] First, the security interest can best be achieved by removing almost all troop presence, closing most bases, abandoning all independent combat operations, and limiting remaining military presence to CT operations conducted by special operations forces and/or intelligence operatives, as well as military assistance and training conducted by regular military forces (the number of forces must be sufficient for their own security — probably 9,000-12,000[28]). To maintain enough presence to prevent Afghanistan from failing or China/Russia/Iran from pursuing unacceptable policies will require some form of ongoing military assistance program to go along with the robust Embassy and CT activities, but it cannot be so expensive and visible as to be rejected by U.S. or Afghan public opinion. If a viable Bilateral Security Agreement (BSA) cannot be negotiated to provide sufficient protections for those remaining forces, then the United States must negotiate a transitional BSA that will cover them partially until such time as they are withdrawn, or *in extremis*, keep them there in the absence of a BSA, an unlikely proposition.

Second, the process of rebuilding Afghanistan must continue if it is not to become a haven from which Violent Extremist Organizations (VEOs) can threaten the world again. Yet, there is little appetite in the West for continued engagement in Afghanistan beyond the bare minimum required to ensure important national security interests. This loss of appetite is partly due to the long duration of the Afghan War and partly due to the widespread corruption and ineptitude of the Afghan government — it is hard to imagine a continued funding stream of any significance after the bulk of American and NATO forces withdraw. This reality produces a policy conundrum in that we must prepare to both reduce our involvement and signal unequivocally that we are doing so, while at the same time take clear steps to indicate a significant ongoing presence in the region. We recommend that our diplomatic presence in Afghanistan and the region be reduced and become more regular, but that U.S. policymakers resist the temptation to draw down economic investment and aid as rapidly, as those tools of policy[29] allow us to bolster the Afghan government and also allow us to compete with other major powers there.

A related conundrum is that continued economic and political development assistance to and through the Afghan national government is required if that government is ever to mature and political practices are to become institutionalized, but the creation of a strong central government for Afghanistan is a poor fit for its natural social contours or its historical models of governance.[30] That is, the model of government envisioned by the Bonn Accords and created by Afghanistan (with U.S. assistance) in 2003 and 2004 is fatally flawed and exacerbates the problems of poor service delivery, ineptitude, and corruption rather than curing or mitigating those political pathologies, although such a system does allow outside powers to better "game" certain political outcomes in Kabul. While a more localized system of government[31] would probably be better for Afghanistan, it is probably not possible for the United States to manage such a transformation even as it is reducing its resources and involvement there. At best, we can probably focus on low-key institutional development. A relevant model here would be the long-running Peace Corps program that has had such a positive effect in many countries—including Afghanistan—for U.S. interests.

The first two pillars to the strategy will not address the last two national interests remaining for the United States in Afghanistan—namely, to prevent a regional power struggle between rival powers that could lead to regional instability, and in particular to prevent the eruption of a regional conflict between nuclear powers; and to potentially prevent the rise of a regional power or alliance of powers whose interests run counter to U.S interests. Nor is there a clear-cut strategy that can be pursued that will have a good chance of achieving these interests. Nonetheless, we recommend that the United States at least regionalize its approach to Afghanistan. The key, as already outlined, will be to maintain enough presence to be able to prevent a regional war between rivals in and around Afghanistan, while disengaging the bulk of our combat forces already present in Afghanistan and reducing the size and footprint of our diplomatic mission there. Wielding the diplomatic scalpel deftly to manipulate regional actors to our own ends is fraught with peril, but probably necessary. A major challenge, however, is that the U.S. Government structures its foreign and national security policy apparatus around country teams and regional desks. Afghanistan sits at the juncture of four regions—East Asia (because of China), Central Asia, South Asia, and the Middle East—and there is no institutional arrangement within the U.S. Government that ties all of these regions together. The Special Representative for Afghanistan and Pakistan position that was created in the State Department in 2009 is a step in this direction, but the position is housed within only one department of the executive branch and only focuses on two of the relevant countries. Moreover, illustrating the broader bureaucratic problem, the State Department still maintains regional bureaus and country teams that dominate the policy and operational environment for the relevant countries. What is required is a change in attitude and organization to achieve U.S. interests concerning Afghanistan.

That is, the United States may have to go beyond a regional approach and globalize its approach to Afghanistan. We propose an institutional reform to the

U.S. national security structure to allow for a global grand strategy to be developed by an interagency cell within the National Security Council. Personnel seconded to this cell should represent relevant national security agencies and departments, as well as draw on academics from universities and think tanks. Those strategists that work in this entity will be tasked with not only developing a grand strategy, but also recommending strategic adjustments to the National Security Adviser and President as the strategy develops. What they must master is not only an understanding of how major rivals pursue their interests in a global context, but how the United States can weave together and wield all of its tools of national power in an effective way to counter the strategies of rivals as they play out around the world.[32]

A last strategy consideration has to do with sustainable governance in Afghanistan. The U.S. approach to extricating itself from protracted limited wars has centered on security assistance, other institutional reform, and state-building more generally. Inevitably, the United States has to become deeply involved with indigenous politicians and their support networks to make such an approach work. In post-9/11 Afghanistan, this involvement was especially intrusive, as the strategy called for not only picking winners and losers, but also constructing an entirely new Afghan political, economic, and social institutional framework.

This political reconstruction occurred in one of the most localized societies on the planet, where the concept of "all politics is local" describes the reality of political life for most people. The political reality of Afghanistan is that an Afghan's identity significantly revolves around a local environ and/or identity group. For most of its history, Afghanistan had a central government that could not intrude very heavily into the countryside, as strong centrifugal social and political forces existed in an uneasy balance with the tenuous authority of the central government. Afghanistan's social order today remains profoundly tilted toward the local, even as the large diaspora population of Afghans in the West is now connected with relatives back home to an extent that has never before existed in human history. Thus, the profound localism may be changing under our feet.[33]

Afghanistan's population is characterized by deep and multifaceted cleavages. People are divided basically along ethnic and linguistic lines, but sectarian, tribal, and racial divisions also exist, and all of these are reinforced by a spatial pattern of population distribution into different regions of the country. That level of complexity does not even do justice to the reality, which is that every village, district, and region of the country are different. The localized country means that the religious framework is based on a syncretic blend of various interpretations of Islamic doctrine with local customs, making the country simultaneously unified by one faith and divided by hundreds of variations on its practice.[34] In a country where tribal social groupings still exist, the social system is based on communal loyalties and emphasizes the local over higher-order identity formations. The rugged topographical features and geographical position of Afghanistan, coupled with its lack of economic development, isolate it internationally and magnify the distance of its people from the government. Often these factors combine to reinforce each other, other times they overlap each other, but collectively they create a complex foundation for modern Afghan politics.

The post-9/11 political reconstruction was further shaped by the reality that Afghanistan's traditional ruler, King Zahir Shah, had been absent from Afghanistan since 1973 while his fellow Durrani Pashtuns had been marginalized during much of that period. Much of the rest of the Pashtun population had participated on one side or another of the long Afghan War of the 1980s and 1990s, and by 9/11 most Pashtuns were in the Taliban camp, as that movement had become something of a political vehicle for Pashtun national aspirations. Positioned in opposition was a fractious alliance of mostly minority ethnic groups from the center and north of the country (hence the "Northern Alliance").

The United States leveraged Northern Alliance militias and their warlord commanders to topple the Taliban government in 2001, while simultaneously picking Durrani Pashtun Hamid Karzai to put a Pashtun face on what would otherwise be a government dominated by northern minority leaders. Karzai's subsequent election victories allowed him to remain the face of the Afghanistan government, even as widespread, endemic corruption undermined its legitimacy to those in the population not directly benefitting from his rule. Moreover, Karzai worked over the past decade to limit the prospects of any challengers to his position, meaning that there are few subordinate leaders from the Pashtun ethnic group that even have a unified Pashtun following (hard to achieve anyway given that ethnicity's tribal makeup).

The United States continues to emphasize institutional development, especially of the Afghan National Security Forces, which the U.S. military continues to train and assist to fight a largely Pashtun insurgency. This means that the United States has few good indigenous options in Afghanistan through which to pursue its strategy.

Constraints and Risks.

In post-2014 Afghanistan, the United States cannot afford to fail to ensure regional stability and forestall rising peer competitors from gaining too much influence in the region. Significant constraints and risks exist. In the short term, Afghanistan is about to undergo a major political transition, as post-Taliban President Hamid Karzai finishes his second term in office in 2014 and will have to give way to a new President (unless he pulls off some political legerdemain that allows him to extend his stay in the Presidential Palace beyond the constitutionally mandated limit). The presidential election of April 2014 (the first ballot) and June 2014 (the second ballot, or runoff) provided an opportunity to change the way Afghanistan has been governed since 2001, and perhaps even find a way to end the long civil war that has tortured the country.[35] Or maybe not. The runoff election between the two largest vote getters—Abdullah Addullah and Ashraf Ghani, ended in acrimony and finger pointing, as Abdullah and his supporters made strong complaints of substantial electoral fraud, calling into question the validity of the election. As noted previously, the political system given form by the 2004 Constitution does not fit Afghan society. No matter which candidate emerges as the next president of Afghanistan, if the election is to be anything other than a rearrangement of the deck chairs on the *Titanic*, important political, economic, and social reforms will need to be implemented. In particular, a way must be found to localize governance, reduce exorbitant corruption, and accommodate the aspirations of Afghanistan's increasingly globalized youth for social change.

Second, the regional multipolar power struggle means that all actors will continue to pursue their interests inside and around Afghanistan, probably using intelligence agents and assets and proxy forces, especially if the United States and NATO troops remain in any sizable force. This reality means that a successful reconciliation and reintegration process with the various factions of the Taliban is virtually impossible to achieve so long as the Taliban remain somewhat of a proxy for Pakistan. Given the growing Indian relationship with and presence in Afghanistan and the ties by ethnicity, sectarianism, and/or money between other regional countries with other proxies inside Afghanistan, it is extremely difficult to imagine Pakistan giving up its proxy.

Exacerbating this problem are the growing global Great Power rivalries between the United States and both a rising China and a resurgent Russia, which are playing out in multiple arenas by way of many actors and various strategies. For example, China's greater assertiveness in the East and South China Sea has prompted the United States to pivot to the Pacific, or vice versa, depending upon your point of view. Likewise, China's increasing pursuit of resources in the Middle East, Africa, and Latin America has collided with American national security interests in those regions, especially (for example) the Syrian civil war and Iran's pursuit of nuclear weapons. Russia's revanchist annexation of Crimea, the 2008 war with Georgia, and support for the Bashar Al-Assad regime in Syria all illustrate a return to a Cold War-style expectation of Great Power status within its immediate neighborhood that collides with American aspirations for a peaceful European Union.

Another complication is that long-term and large-scale Western military presence in Afghanistan cannot be contemplated, given the difficulty in securing an adequate BSA between Afghanistan and the United States. Also operating as significant constraints are the limits imposed by the economic recession in Europe and the United States, the pervasive war-weariness on both sides of the Atlantic, the widespread perception that the oft-stated military goals for the Afghan War have been achieved, and the persistent regional and local interests that diverge from and threaten America's military presence and interests.

Finally, all of the foregoing suggests that any substantial American withdrawal or disengagement from Afghanistan will lead to a deepening of the civil war already underway there. The Taliban will not be the only proxy for a regional power, nor will Pakistan's Inter-Services Intelligence Directorate be the only intelligence service to play a role inside Afghanistan. As already noted, a civil war in Afghanistan now threatens to unhinge the region in a way that the war of the 1990s never could. Should an Afghan civil war cause regional instability, U.S. interests will be harmed, especially if such a war were to widen or turn into a general or nuclear war.

Conclusion.

The United States started this century in its traditional position of ignoring Afghanistan. The events of 9/11 forced the United States to change that position. America's longest war has taken place since then on Afghan soil, and that war in concert with the long war in Iraq and the military operations elsewhere against Islamist terrorists have combined to produce deep war-weariness among the American public. Few Americans have any desire to remain engaged in Afghanistan to any extent after the planned withdrawal of American forces concludes in 2014. However, the historical lesson provided by the American decision to turn its attention away from the region following the Soviet withdrawal in 1989 that ultimately led to the rise of the Taliban and fostering of al-Qaeda, combined with the multipolar power struggle in the region, mean that the United States cannot afford to fully disengage from Afghanistan again. Thus, the American withdrawal will most likely follow the strategy guidance laid out previously — namely, the CT organizations will continue to conduct activities in the region, from which Afghanistan will provide a logical platform; the customary diplomatic and foreign assistance approaches of the U.S. government, especially the security assistance programs, will continue, both to provide the platform for the CT operators and presence for the United States vis-à-vis its regional rivals; and American intelligence and military assets that can monitor and tamp down the risks of regional instability in a nuclear fault zone will also continue.

Afghanistan's place in the American consciousness will necessarily fade, hopefully, as the United States moves to draw down its presence and involvement there. As with all limited wars, however, it is difficult to declare the Afghan War a victory. Objectives achieved fall mostly in the category of possible prevention of further terrorist attacks, and those successes (if any) came by way of costly strategies that were intertwined with America's war in Iraq and operations against Islamist terrorists. The very exit strategy from Afghanistan is reminiscent of the "Vietnamization" strategy of an earlier era[36] and dangerously flawed thereby because when the United States finally pulled out of Vietnam, there was no stomach to go back in if the South Vietnamese troops needed help; hence, that strategy quickly failed.[37] Thus, even the limited, low-key approach suggested here is risky in the current political and economic climate of the United States, meaning that it is possible that the United States will set aside any reasonable strategy to achieve its legitimate national security interests in the Afghanistan region after 2014.

ENDNOTES

1. Strategy models typically distinguish between national interests, policy ends, and strategic objectives, but all of these terms refer to similar concepts—namely, the goal that a country attempts to pursue or achieve. In this monograph, we will use national interests in order to refer to national goals.

2. National interests vary in intensity. The U.S. Army War College strategy model suggests that the most significant interests can be classified as "survival," which, because of their essential importance to the nation, typically must be secured through public expenditures and even military might. Interests of great significance that still typically require action are "vital." Interests of lesser significance can be classified as "important," while those interests of even lesser significance can be classified as "peripheral." This continuum can be found at Alan G. Stolberg, "Crafting National Interests in the 21st Century," J. Boone Bartholomees, Jr., ed., *The U.S. Army War College Guide to National Security Issues—Volume II: National Security Policy and Strategy*, 5th Ed., Carlisle, PA: Strategic Studies Institute, U.S. Army War College, 2010, p. 19.

3. Early post-9/11 strategy debate suggest that at least some U.S. officials had multiple targets in mind in what would come to be known as a Global War on Terror (GWOT). See Bob Woodward, *Plan of Attack*, New York: Simon and Schuster, 2004.

4. H. Richard Yarger, "Toward a Theory of Strategy: Art Lykke and the U.S. Army War College Strategy Model," J. Boone Bartholomees, Jr., ed., *The U.S. Army War College Guide to National Security Issues – Volume I: Theory of War and Strategy*, 5th Ed., Carlisle, PA: Strategic Studies Institute, U.S. Army War College, 2012, p. 50.

5. Many scholars believe that this use of the term "nation-building" is inaccurate, misleading, and/or insulting, preferring "state-building" instead. In the Afghanistan and Iraq context, nation-building came to mean the international (U.S.-led) effort to replace or rebuild state institutions in the wake of invasion and occupation. See James Dobbins, Seth G. Jones, Keith Crane, and Beth Cole DeGrasse, *The Beginner's Guide to Nation-Building*, Santa Monica, CA: RAND Corporation, 2007. Also see Francis Fukuyama, ed., *Nation-building: Beyond Afghanistan and Iraq*, Baltimore, MD: Johns Hopkins University Press, 2006. We use the term deliberately here, not only because it was the term of choice in the early days of the Afghanistan and Iraq interventions, but also because it had been a celebrated issue in the 2000 presidential election.

6. Larry P. Goodson, "Building Democracy after Conflict: Bullets, Ballots, and Poppies in Afghanistan," *Journal of Democracy*, Vol. 16, No. 1, January 2005, pp. 24-38.

7. Security Sector Reform was envisioned as part of the Bonn Accords of December 2001 and took shape out of the Tokyo Donors Conference of January 2002. Five key sectors were identified, with a lead nation taking primary responsibility for each sector: the United States was the lead country in charge of the development of the new Afghan military, Germany in charge of the development of the police forces, Italy in charge of the justice sector, the United Kingdom (UK) in charge of counter narcotics, and Japan responsible for the Disarmament, Demobilization, and Reintegration Process.

8. By 2006, the United States had taken over as the lead nation for the development of the police forces and justice reform.

9. In Islam, a defensive jihad results when the *Umma* (Muslim population) perceives itself to be threatened by an outside party or force. See Thomas H. Johnson and W. Chris Mason, "Under-

standing the Taliban and Insurgency in Afghanistan," *Orbis: A Journal of World Affairs*, Vol. 51, No. 1, 2007, pp. 71-89.

10. We conceive of this as a modern-day Great Game, a popular term to describe the 19th century competition by imperial Great Britain and Russia for influence in Central Asia between their two expansionist empires. This term is widely accepted; for example, see Peter Hopkirk, *The Great Game: On Secret Service in High Asia*, London, UK: John Murray, 2006. The Russians referred to the same concept by the label, Tournament of Shadows; see Karl Ernest Meyer and Shareen Blair Brysac, *Tournament of Shadows: The Great Game and the Race for Empire in Central Asia*, New York: Basic Books, 2006. Not all scholars agree with the concept, such as Benjamin D. Hopkins, *The Making of Modern Afghanistan*, London, UK: Palgrave/Macmillan, 2008. Other scholars and policy analysts accept the existence of the concept, but do not think it has application, even metaphorical, to the present situation. In the 19th century, an expansionist colonial Great Britain (from India) and an expansionist imperial Russia collided in Inner Asia as the former pushed north and the latter pushed south. High mountain ranges and barren deserts forced both powers to "play" what came to be known as the "Great Game" by the creative use of spies ("diplomacy by intrigue") and local forces ("war by proxy"). This "light footprint" approach generally limited the exposure to both powers, although Great Power competition continued until the early decades of the 20th century. Great Britain declined from its global position at the end of World War II and withdrew from the Indian subcontinent. The United States inherited Great Britain's role, but did not choose to compete fully with Russia's successor—the Soviet Union—in the Inner Asian cockpit of Afghanistan, until the 1979 Soviet invasion there presented the United States with an opportunity to bleed the Soviets. The unexpected collapse of the Soviet Union in 1991 following its ignominious withdrawal from Afghanistan in 1989 and the nearly simultaneous turning away from the region by the United States during the 1990s allowed the first multipolar configuration in the region to develop in over a century. The 9/11 attacks ignited further changes in the region that have now led to a complex situation unlike anything in recent memory, but we believe it exhibits some features that are reminiscent of the earlier Great Game period.

11. See Alexander Cooley, *Great Games, Local Rules: The New Great Power Contest in Central Asia*, New York: Oxford, 2012. Also see Nicola Contessi's recent review article, "Central Eurasia and the New Great Game: Players, Moves, Outcomes, and Scholarship," *Asian Security*, Vol. 9, No. 3, September-December 2013, pp. 231-241.

12. "On Eve of Afghan Election, Waning U.S. Support for War," *ABC News/Washington Post Poll*, August 19, 2009, available from *abcnews.go.com/images/PollingUnit/1093a2Afghanistan.pdf*.

13. Scott Clement, "Majority of Americans Say Afghan War Has Not Been Worth Fighting, Post-ABC News Poll Finds," *Washington Post*, December 19, 2013.

14. German Marshall Fund of the United States, *Transatlantic Trends: Key Findings 2012*, pp. 35-36, available from *trends.gmfus.org/files/2012/09/TT-2012-Key-Findings-Report.pdf*. Surveys of Afghans reveal that security concerns are very significant (as of 2013), but that confidence in the Afghan National Army had increased dramatically by then, as well. See, for example, Keith Shawe, *Afghanistan in 2013: A Survey of the Afghan People*, Kabul, Afghanistan: The Asia Foundation, 2013.

15. German Marshall Fund of the United States, *Transatlantic Trends*, p. 34.

16. Hillary Clinton, "America's Pacific Century," *Foreign Policy*, Vol. 189, November 2011, pp. 56-63.

17. Kautilya, *The Arthashashtra*, L. N. Rangarajan, ed., rearranged, trans., and introduced, New Delhi, India: Penguin Books India, 1992.

18. This may pose a significant challenge to the acceptability test of strategy, unless our definition of acceptable has changed.

19. Pervez Musharraf, *In the Line of Fire: A Memoir*, New York: Free Press, 2006.

20. "Drone Wars Pakistan: Analysis," Washington, DC: New America Foundation, available from *securitydata.newamerica.net/ drones/pakistan/analysis.*

21. At least six significant policy concerns exist when the United States undertakes light footprint warfare. First, such approaches may prove insufficient to the task; that is, drone strikes, targeted killings, cyber warfare—all may prove ineffective in the face of a strong state actor prepared to fight back from its sovereign territory. Second, such approaches may not be sustainable and/or viable over time. Related to the foregoing concern, such approaches may also have limited political legitimacy with the American people, who must be informed in order to check abuses of power by the executive branch or the government at large. A fourth concern is the blowback that such approaches produce. Fifth, proliferation is another significant concern. Finally, there is the issue of precedent. We might be establishing an international norm that condones the violation of national sovereignty to kill "terrorists" or "combatants," and the collateral damage necessary to conduct those strikes. Such techniques could be used against Americans, or against American drone controllers. None of these policy concerns invalidate the use of light footprint technologies or techniques of war, but in concert with the legal concerns they do raise some red flags.

22. Alberto R, Gonzales, "Drones: The Power to Kill," *The George Washington Law Review*, Vol. 82, No. 1, pp. 1-57.

23. In May 2013, in a much-publicized major policy speech, President Obama argued that the United States could not slip into this form of shadow war. See Barack Obama, "Remarks by the President at the National Defense University," May 23, 2013, available from *www.whitehouse.gov/the-press-office/2013/05/23/ remarks-president-national-defense-university.* In the 6 months following that speech, however, although the pace of lethal U.S. drone strikes in Pakistan and Yemen decreased, the overall casualties produced by those strikes increased, compared to the 6-month period prior to the speech. See Jack Serle, "Drone Strikes in Yemen: New Analysis Questions Constraint on US Drone Strikes," *The Bureau of Investigative Journalism*, November 25, 2013, available from *www.thebureauinvestigates.com/2013/11/26/new-analysis-questions-constraint-on-us-drone-strikes/.*

24. U.S. Department of Defense, *Quadrennial Defense Review 2014*, March 4, 2014, Washington, U.S. Department of Defense, available from *www.defense.gov/pubs/2014_Quadrennial_Defense_Review.pdf*.

25. As well as India, which signed the 123 Agreement in 2006 that allows for the transfer of sensitive nuclear materials and knowledge to India by the United States (and others), but only for civilian purposes.

26. NATO, *International Security Assistance Force: Key Facts and Figures*, December 1, 2013, Brussels, Belgium, available from *www.isaf.nato.int/images/stories/File/2013-12-01%20ISAF%20 Placemat-final.pdf*.

27. On April 30, 1975, North Vietnamese forces took Saigon (now Ho Chi Minh City), ending the long Vietnam war. U.S. citizens and pro-American South Vietnamese were evacuated in the face of the oncoming troops, and on the last possible day, numerous helicopter flights took people from the U.S. Embassy and residential buildings to waiting U.S. naval ships in the South China Sea. A famous photograph came to symbolize the American loss in Vietnam.

28. CBS News, "Pentagon Eyes 10,000 Troops for Afghanistan, or None," January 22, 2014, available from *www.cbsnews. com/news/pentagon-eyes-10000-troops-for-afghanistan-or-none/*.

29. The general tools of foreign policy are often characterized as the diplomatic, information, military, and economic (DIME) model. We propose that this model be redefined, where the "I" stands for intelligence instead of "information," as the intelligence tool has been important to our Afghan strategy to date. Thus far, our strategy has been heavy on the military and intelligence tools, with less emphasis on the diplomatic tool and even less on the economic tool, dIMe. We recommend a restructuring of how much weight we put on these tools, such that diplomacy and economics become dominant, while the intelligence and military tools slip into the background, DimE. Using this redefined acronym, the strategy might be explained as:

To maintain enough presence to prevent Afghanistan from failing or China/Russia/Iran from pursuing unacceptable policies will require some form of ongoing military assistance program to go along with the robust Embassy and CT activities, but it cannot be so expensive and visible as to be rejected by public opinion;

To continue the destruction of Al Qa'ida, a limited CT approach is required, employ direct action against high-value targets that threaten the United States (directly or regional U.S. interests);

Use the military and intelligence community to monitor nuclear weapons and asymmetric actors, in particular to prevent the India-Pakistan rivalry from erupting into open conflict again;

Invest enough diplomatic and foreign assistance capital to remain engaged in Afghanistan to the extent that the United States can continue to have presence and standing in the region.

30. Known as a unitary system of government, such as in most countries.

31. The two major types are a federal system, such as exists in India or the United Arab Emirates, or a confederal system, such as the United States had under the Articles of Confederation.

32. For example, China's actions in international organizations, Afghanistan, South China Sea, Myanmar, Persian Gulf, Africa, and Latin America, among other places and venues, can all be considered to be part of one overall strategy. Alternatively, Russia's actions in international organizations, the Ukraine, Moldova, the Caucasus, Syria, and Central Asia, among other places and venues, might also be considered to be part of one overall strategy. To counter either or both, if such is desired, requires an understanding of what can be done where, when, and how, and the impact of a move in one place or venue on other places and venues. Reviewers of this monograph recommended that this proposal be scaled back or eliminated altogether, as running counter to what bureaucratic politics in Washington will allow. We considered doing so, but ultimately felt compelled to leave this

proposal in the monograph, because we do not think the United States can develop a successful approach to the region anchored by Afghanistan without globalizing our strategy.

33. Larry P. Goodson, "Picking Up the Pieces," *Hoover Digest*, Vol. 1, 2002, pp. 57-67.

34. Thomas H. Johnson, "Religious Figures, Insurgency, and Jihad in Southern Afghanistan," *Who Speaks for Islam?: Muslim Grassroots Leaders and Popular Preachers in South Asia*, NBR Special Report #22, Seattle, WA: The National Bureau of Asian Research, February 2010, pp. 41- 65.

35. However, the ethnic and political currents of Afghanistan have swirled together over time in such a way that a Pashtun must lead the country, as both history and the fact that the Pashtuns are the largest ethnic group mean that they expect to rule the country. The two vice-presidential spots are doled out to ethnic minority candidates in a blatant effort to secure votes from the important minority groups. Thus, all of the top candidates in the 2014 presidential election can claim Pashtun heritage and have minority group running mates. The frontrunners also each have a strong additional feature to their candidacies. Former Foreign Minister Abdullah Abdullah has long been a leader of the Tajik-dominated Northern Alliance and has a large campaign chest to draw upon. Karzai's brother, Qayum Karzai, along with former National Security Adviser Zalmay Rassoul, both hope that Karzai will endorse their candidacies, which might prove decisive. In the unlikely event that the balloting is anywhere close to free and fair, former Finance Minister Ashraf Ghani is popular among Afghanistan's many young people for his willingness to move beyond the age of the warlords. If warlords can still rule, however, both former Defense Minister Abdul Rahim Wardak and Member of Parliament Abdul Rassoul Sayyaf would fit the bill. Whoever finally wins (the election is a two-ballot affair) will find overcoming the ethnic divisions (the Pashtuns distrust the Tajiks and no one trusts the Pashtuns) and breaking the cycle of corruption that has become such a feature of the Afghan government extremely difficult.

36. Thomas H. Johnson and W. Chris Mason, "Refighting the Last War: Afghanistan and the Vietnam Template," *Military Review*, November-December, 2009, pp. 2-14.

37. Henry Kissinger, *Diplomacy*, New York: Simon and Schuster, 1995, pp. 692-700.

U.S. ARMY WAR COLLEGE

Major General William E. Rapp
Commandant

*****

STRATEGIC STUDIES INSTITUTE
and
U.S. ARMY WAR COLLEGE PRESS

Director
Professor Douglas C. Lovelace, Jr.

Director of Research
Dr. Steven K. Metz

Authors
Dr. Larry P. Goodson
Dr. Thomas H. Johnson

Editor for Production
Dr. James G. Pierce

Publications Assistant
Ms. Rita A. Rummel

*****

Composition
Mrs. Jennifer E. Nevil

www.ingramcontent.com/pod-product-compliance
Lightning Source LLC
Chambersburg PA
CBHW071127280526
45787CB00003B/1208